30 POEMS OF LOVE,

LOVE POEMS TO GOD

Table of Contents

DEDICATION

I dedicate this book of poems to my beloved son, Caleb Spencer Funcherss. My son inspires me to reach for the stars. Love you and let's keep dreaming! Lots of ♥, Mommy.

1

RESURRECTION

Through the resurrecting power of Jesus, your spiritual house is renovated

Through the resurrecting power of Jesus, your soul is remodeled

Through the resurrecting power of Jesus, your body is redesigned

Commentary: Jesus made the ultimate sacrifice by dying on the cross and resurrecting from the grave. For those who dedicate their life to Jesus Christ, their relationship with God can be renovated, remodeled, and redesigned. As the relationship with God becomes more intimate, the followers of Jesus Christ desire to study and apply the written word of God in every area of their life. Decisions about the mind, body, and soul are transformed as believers step out on faith and obey God.

2

TRINITY

Pour your life-giving word on your people God

Deliver our souls from dehydration Jesus

Quench our hearts Holy Spirit

Let us drink from the fountain of life

Commentary: God, your children desire an intimate relationship with you. We are hungry for your life-giving word, thirsty for deliverance, and famished for your presence. The menu of the Holy

Trinity is nourishment and life for those who partake it.

3

HOLY SPIRIT

Erupt within us Holy Spirit

Burn bright within us Holy Spirit

Glow within us Holy Spirit

Blaze within us Holy Spirit

Ignite our spirits

Commentary: The presence of God lives within his children. Spend time with your heavenly Father, so the Holy Spirit can erupt within you. When God's family enters a room, the Holy Spirit burns bright around them. The blaze of righteousness is contagious. There is a glowing light surrounding the family of Christ that can be utilized to spread the gospel.

4

S.W.

Submit

Pray

Invite

Receive

Insist

Treasure

Understanding

Angels

Love

Worship

Acknowledge

Repent

Commentary: Submit to the authority of the living God and pray to him with an open heart. My family in Christ, invite the holy spirit into your life and awaken the power of God. Insist on believing in God's promises and the treasures of heaven will overtake you. Understand, my brothers and sisters, that God is the supreme protector and has assigned angels for protection. Display God's love to the world and worship him regardless of the circumstances. Acknowledge mistakes and ask God for forgiveness.

5

WALK IN LOVE

Walk in love

Give way to the hearts-locked

Let love overflow

Walk in love

Let chains fall

Let love overflow

Walk in love

Collapse every wall

Let love overflow

Walk in love

Let open the cage door

Let love overflow

Commentary: God has breathed life and unconditional love in our hearts, share it with the world. The key of love has unlocked the chains around closed hearts. Regardless of our hurts, disappointments, and pain, love has made the wall around our heart collapse. Because of God's love, we can forgive and walk in love.

6

LOVE WITHOUT LIMITS

Love as bright as the sun

Love as colorful as the rainbow

Love as loud as thunder

Love as deep as the ocean

Love as much as you can

Commentary: You are a walking testimony of God's love because the love within you radiates as bright as the sun. There are many layers, dimensions, and complexities to loving people but build a relationship with them and exhibit your colorful approach to love, forgiveness, acceptance, and tolerance. Christians love for people is thunderous and powerful because we pray blessings for our enemies. Reach deep within God's power and love unconditionally.

7

WALK INTO

Walk into God's sacrificial love

Walk into God's redemptive power

Walk into God's protective arms

Walk into God's eternal goodness

Walk into God's unmerited favor

Walk into God's sudden promotion

Walk into God's holy presence

Walk into God's still peace

Walk into God's contagious joy

Walk into God's loving correction

Walk into God's gracious generosity

Walk into God's immeasurable prosperity

Walk into God's infinite wisdom

Walk into God's best life for you

Commentary: The creator of the universe arms is wide open ready to receive those who desire him. God desires to wrap his loving arms around those who seek him. Walk into God's sacrificial, unconditional love, and the results will be amazing.

8

PURPOSE

Inject your purpose into my heart

Insert your purpose into my mind

Introduce your purpose into my actions

Feed your purpose into my body

Engulf your purpose into my decisions

Commentary: God has designed us for a reason, and there are no coincidences in the Kingdom of God. Building an intimate relationship with God will reveal your personalized plan from God. Your personalized plan from God will include your purpose. Embrace and implant your purpose in your heart, mind, actions, body, and decisions.

9

GUARANTEED

deliverance GUARANTEED

influence GUARANTEED

WISDOM guaranteed

FAVOR guaranteed

healing GUARANTEED

comfort GUARANTEED

GUIDANCE guaranteed

GROWTH guaranteed

God is the only GUARANTEE

Commentary: Accepting Jesus Christ as Lord, is the only guarantee to have access to the Father. Building an intimate relationship with God is the only guarantee to the inheritance from the creator of the world.

10

OPEN DOORS

Close the door on sin

Open the door of life

Close the door on doubt

Open the door of faith

Close the door on fear

Open the door on love

Close the door on strife

Open the door of love

Commentary: For those who desire an encounter with God, the door to life is open. With a sincere heart, repent of sins and open the door of faith. Spend quality time with God daily to understand his character. God's perfect love slams the door on doubt, fear, and strife.

11

WAGING

Waging war on people with my tongue

Waging death on people with my tongue

Waging sin on my life with my tongue

Forgive me, Father

Turn my tongue around, Father

Waging peace on people with my tongue

Waging life on people with my tongue

Waging obedience on my life with my tongue

Commentary: The spoken word is powerful and has the power to change the environment and hearts in a positive or negative way. Guard your tongue and promote the best news, the gospel of Jesus Christ.

12

BENEFITS

Love, mercy, forgiveness, protection,

understanding

Love, mercy, forgiveness, protection,

understanding

Love, mercy, forgiveness, protection,

understanding

Best benefit package in the world!

Commentary: Christians have the ultimate dream job, promoting God's benefits! God's family business provides access to the best benefits package in the world; love, mercy, forgiveness, and understanding.

13

IN THIS HOUSE

We obey God in this house

In this house, we are healed

We are leaders in this house

In this house, we love

We forgive in this house

In this house, we pray

We serve the Lord in this house

Commentary: As a family unit, we decided to follow and listen to God's instructions. We are surrendering control of our lives to God. Since we made these decisions, God's love is manifesting through us. The favor of God is running rampant in our household; healing, leadership, forgiveness, and service.

14

HE IS EVERYWHERE

He is in the front

He is in the back

He is on the top

He is on the bottom

He is on the left

He is on the right

God surrounds us with his love

Commentary: Regardless of the direction that his children travel in life, God's love surrounds them.

He speaks to hearts and witnesses to the inner core. God's presence surrounds us always.

15

FOR YOU

Everything is for you because you made the ultimate sacrifice to restore our relationship

Everything is for you because you have invited me to your table for a feast

Everything is for you because you forgive me when I mess up and remember it no more

Everything is for you because you are always on time rescuing me from harm

Everything is for you because you have written me the greatest love story

Commentary: For those who say "yes" to God's love, decisions and action are to glorify him. Hearts become tender to God when the greatest love story is understood. Acceptance is replaced with inferiority because Almighty God has provided a dinner invitation, to be in his holy presence. Shackles of condemnation are broken because repentance and forgiveness of sins are available through Christ Jesus. God's perfect timing and protection are a testimony of his unconditional love.

16

WHY

Why would I turn my back on his sweet love?

Why would I walk away from his sweet love?

Why would I give up on his sweet love?

Why, Why, Why

Why would I turn my back on his sweet love?

Why would I walk away from his sweet love?

Why would I give up on his sweet love?

Commentary: God's love is the sweetest and greatest experience. His ultimate expression of love is sacrificing his son, Jesus, on the cross for our sins. As we build a relationship with God, the depths of love expand. Because of his perfect love, let us face him, walk towards him and commit to him.

17

CLAP YOUR HANDS

Clap your hands, my Lord, Clap your hands, my Lord

Make a path to righteousness, walk with me

Open sealed doors to my heart, set me free

Clap your hands, my Lord, Clap your hands, my Lord

Clap your hands, my Lord, Clap your hands, my Lord

Tear down walls of guilt, forgive me

Remove barriers of strife, cleanse my pain

Clap your hands, my Lord, Clap your hands my Lord

Commentary: With God's favor upon us, the impossibilities become the possibilities. God can wiggle his fingers and move mountains to guide us to righteousness. He can forgive and cleanse our souls with a snap of his fingers. Any circumstance can change with a clap of God's hands.

18

GARDEN

Water the seeds of life dormant in your children

Plant your children in fertile ground

Shine your sunlight on your children

Watch over your children's harvest

Bless your children as they blossom

Heavenly Father, thank you for giving us the Garden of Eden on earth

Commentary: Guide your children to their purpose in life, and plant them in the house of the Lord. Shine your spirit upon the church so that the world can witness your glory. Protect your children's blossoming harvest from crows. Thankful to God for planting seeds of purpose and increase in our lives.

19

WATER OF LOVE

Shower me with your grace

Sprinkle me with your favor

Splash me with your protection

Drizzle me with your mercy

Bath me with your wisdom

Cleanse me with your forgiveness

Cascade me with your love

Commentary: Open our heart and receive the generous promises of God. Let the rivers of grace, favor, and protection flow through our lives. Rain mercy, wisdom, and forgiveness upon us God. Feel the waves of the heavenly Father's love.

20

TAKING COVER

Swim through the ocean of blessings

Take cover from the storms of life

Sail on the rivers of love

Take cover from the storms of life

Surf along the sea of forgiveness

Take cover from the storms of life

Dip into the pool of prosperity

Take cover from the storms of life

Kayak to the lake of courage

Take cover from the storms of life

Commentary: God has predicted a stormy forecast occurring at some point in your life, but he has provided his family with protection and courage. During the challenging seasons, seek shelter in God's love and forgiveness. When the storm passes, you will experience blessings and prosperity.

21

WITH GOD

With God, you can weather any storm of life

With God, you sail smoothly through the choppy sea of life

With God, you float gracefully through the trails of life

God's peace is always with you

Commentary: Challenges are expected and no match for God's children because God has provided a battle plan. Our ammunition is the

living word of God, the bible. Enclosed in the
spiritual battle plan is a strategy to win every
battle. God's army has the peaceful reassurance
that victory belongs to them.

22

POWER SOURCE

Plug into the power of God,

Let the current flow through you

Plug into the power of God,

Let the light shine bright in you

Plug into the power of God,

Let him be your source that never short circuits

Plug into the power of God,

Let his source of power guide you in the darkness

Commentary: Submit your heart to God and declare that Jesus is Lord of your life. Invite the presence of God into your life and embrace the power of the holy spirit, the light. Flash your light on darkness and give the world hope. God's power never fails or short-circuit.

23

YOU ARE

You are my rock; you give me strength to handle any challenges that come my way

You are my GPS; you navigate me in the right direction when I'm lost

You are my blanket; you cover me from harm

You are my anchor; you keep me steady in the moving sea

All things are possible with you, through you and by you!

Commentary: God's presence manifests in variou ways. He provides strength, guidance, and protection during crisis. Because our God's character is consistent and trustworthy, his children's faith is unshakable.

24

BREAKTHROUGH

The dam is shaking

The dam is rumbling

The dam's foundation is cracking

The dam's barrier is breaking

The overflow of water is rushing abundantly

The breakthrough of God's favor has been released in my life

Commentary: Fear is attempting to shake and rumble the soul of God's children. Doubt is failing to crack and break the spirits of God's children. The overflow of God's abundance is gushing into the lives of God's children.

25

ROCK CLIMBING

As I rock climb through life, my endurance and strength will be put to the test

As I rock climb through life, I must dig into the mountain of God's word

As I rock climb through life, I tightly hold on to the rope of faith

As I rock climb through life, I am climbing higher and higher to the cave of righteousness

Commentary: In life, circumstances will test our faith. When those challenges arise, dig into God's word and hold on tight to the rope of faith. God is preparing our endurance and strength for our next assignment and blessings.

26

ORCHESTRA

God is the master conductor of life

He is conducting and positioning the musicians to play in harmony, tempo and to make beautiful music

He is preparing the musicians to perform in venues all over the world

In God's orchestra, no venue is off limits

Commentary: God is conducting everything in heaven and earth. He is the master of all life and all things. He determines the beats and rhythm of life. To proclaim the good news of Jesus Christ, God's family band must prepare by building a relationship with him. He is preparing his family band to sing about the gospel all over the world.

27

GOD IS

God is my uber driver, driving me to my destination

God is my mail carrier, always delivering me

God is my pilot, flying me over turbulence

God is my conductor, saying all aboard

God is my bike, peddling me to victory

God is my skates, rolling me into abundance

God is my boat, sailing me to peace

Commentary: God is everything to everyone who says "yes" to him! In trials and tribulations, God delivers his children to victory. He gently blows peace in our hearts and provides prosperity in every area of our lives.

28

HOLD ON

Hold on; your breakthrough is on its way!

Hold on; it is like a volcano about to erupt.

Hold on; your breakthrough is on its way!

Hold on, can't you feel the tremors?

Hold on; your breakthrough is on its way!

Hold on, hold on, hold on!

Commentary: Hold on to God's love and faith. The promises of God in the spiritual realm is about to erupt in the physical realm. In this process of God's promises manifesting from the spiritual realm to the physical realm, faith muscles are tremoring and tired from holding on. Stand on God's word regardless of what the senses are screaming. Quiet and calm the senses by believing in God's unchanging Word.

29

RECIPE

God has created the tastiest recipe for my life

God has provided me with all the ingredients to mix

God is stirring the pot of my spirit

God is baking his love at the right temperature

God is removing the heat at just the right time

Following God's recipe, I will win the baking contest of life

Commentary: God is the master chef in his house. He has the best homemade plan for those who have declared that Jesus is Lord. The Bible contains all the secret ingredients needed for every situation, and his perfect love sustains his children during challenges. Submitting to God's word stirs the spirit to cling closer to him.

30

REACHING

Reaching new levels

Reaching new heights

Reaching new dimensions

Reaching beyond the stars

Reaching beyond the moon

Reaching beyond the sky

Reaching my home

Reaching my neighbors

Reaching my city

Commentary: Reach, stretch, grab on to God's unchanging hand. Deepening your relationship with God will skyrocket your purpose to new levels, new heights, and new dimensions. With this high functioning level of confidence in God, discipleship becomes a reality. Equipping saints to proclaim the gospel of Jesus Christ to the world.

Made in the USA
Lexington, KY
17 November 2019

57179605R00041